W9-ANN-214

The Giraffe

AN EARLY BIRD BOOK™

Written by Margaret Lane
Illustrated by David Wright

Random House New York

The giraffe is the tallest animal in the world. It is gentle in behavior and strangely beautiful. It has hoofs like a cow's, long legs, and a head sort of like a camel's, with large ears and bony tufts on top. But the most amazing thing about the giraffe is its long neck.

Even though food may be hard to find on the African plains, the giraffes eat well. They feed off of leaves from trees that other animals cannot reach. They coil their long black tongues around the twigs of acacias and thorn bushes and pull off the leaves.

Giraffes are not easy to see when they are browsing among trees. Their beautiful patterned hides look like dappled sun and shade. They are safer in a patch of woodland than on the open plain.

Their extraordinarily long necks have another advantage. With their heads held high, the giraffes can see nearly two miles away. They can spot an enemy long before it gets near them. A hunting lioness knows this, and must plan her attack carefully.

Because of their great height, giraffes find it difficult to drink from a water hole. To do this they must spread out their forelegs and stretch down to reach the water. The lioness crouches in the bushes and waits for that moment.

But the giraffe is not without
defense. It has a powerful kick, and
if it is standing upright can stun and
trample an enemy. It can also gallop
faster than any lion and can go without
water for long periods, avoiding
water holes.

The family life of the giraffe is rather casual. The herd is usually composed of cows with a few calves around them. The bulls prefer to live on their own, with occasional company.

The cows give birth to their calves fifteen months after mating, and nurse them for perhaps a year. But the young ones eventually drift away, and many die, or are eaten by lions, before they are fully grown.

Sometimes two bulls will fight before mating with a cow, but their battles are rarely serious. They strike with their heads, swinging their powerful necks, but never kick one another. Kicking is reserved for real enemies such as the prowling hyena and the stalking lion.

The giraffes' favorite feeding times are dawn and dusk. At midday they chew their cud, like a farmyard cow, for about two hours. Then they browse again in the shade. Oxpecker birds perch on the giraffes' necks or shoulders and gobble up pesky ticks.

Apart from lions, the giraffes' only other enemy has been humans. African tribes have hunted them for meat, for their beautiful patterned hides, which make strong leather, and for their tasseled tails, which can be used as fly-whisks. Even today poachers with guns and snares pursue giraffes in game reserves.

leopard

In ancient times giraffes were sent as important presents by Arab rulers to the leaders of other countries. Julius Caesar had one in Rome, where it marched in his triumphal processions. People then believed it to be a cross between a leopard and a camel, and called it *camelopard*.

camel

Nowadays the giraffe is found only in Africa, south of the Sahara, and lives chiefly in nature reserves. It is a great attraction to tourists, and has become quite used to humans and cars. However, people must keep their distance and behave quietly.